The History of the Claddagh Ring:

Learn the Stories, Secrets, and Legends of Ireland's Symbol of Love, A Great Irish Wedding or Anniversary Gift

Mullarkey's Books of Ireland, November 2023

THIS BOOK IS A GIFT...

FROM: _____

TO: _____

LET LOVE AND
FRIENDSHIP REIGN...

The History of the Claddagh Ring:

Learn the Stories, Secrets, and Legends of Ireland's Symbol of Love, A Great Irish Wedding or Anniversary Gift

Paperback: 978-1-960227-85-0

Hardcover: 978-1-960227-84-3

A Very Special Free Bonus!

Do you want to learn more about Ireland?

Interesting and Unusual Ireland can be yours for FREE...
This BONUS book has fascinating trivia, interesting tales and
compelling stories about Ireland that you won't find elsewhere...

DOWNLOAD YOUR COPY <u>FOR FREE</u> SO YOU CAN
LEARN ALL ABOUT IRELAND

Dedication

I dedicate this book to my late mother, Kathleen Mullarkey, who gave me a Claddagh ring when I turned 21. I also dedicate this book to my niece and goddaughter Eabha Slattery, who lives within a gentle stroll of the Claddagh. I hope one day she will cherish that Claddagh ring as her own. Of course, let's not forget Eabha's mother, Maura Mullarkey. She and Eabha are the original "Galway Girls!"

I'd also like to pay tribute to the many fascinating characters in this book, including the Claddagh people and their king, as well as Richard Joyce, and Margaret of the Bridges.

Finally, here's raising a glass to all those who make beautiful Claddagh rings and to all those who wear and treasure Ireland's favorite piece of jewelry.

November 2023

Séamus Mullarkey

Preface

Thank you sincerely for buying this book. I'm delighted you decided to add it to your bookshelf. I was born in Galway, July 21st, 1969, in what was then the Calvary Hospital on the opposite side of Galway Bay to the Claddagh. Although I've traveled far and wide and now live in New York, Galway and everything to do with it, including the Claddagh ring, has remained dear to my heart. Through the years I've enjoyed exchanging facts and folklore about the Claddagh ring with friends and family. They've always seemed very interested in what I have to share, so I decided to gather all the fascinating stories and put them together in one place. Although I do hope my friends will read and enjoy this book, I also wish that readers whom I may never meet will appreciate it and in that way a bond of friendship will grow between us as well.

Again, thanks so much.

Tá súil agam go mbaineann sibh go léir taitneamh as an leabhar seo

Phonetic version:

TAWH SOOHL OGUM GUH WAHHNIEN SHIV GUH LEHR TATNAV AS UHN LOHWAHR SHUH

(Irish for 'I hope you all enjoy this book')

Séamus Mullarkey, November 2023

Table of Contents

"The Old Claddagh Ring"

...excerpt from a poem by Patrick B. Kelly

The old Claddagh ring, sure it was my
grandmother's,

She wore it a lifetime and gave it to me;

All through the long years, she wore it so
proudly.

It was made where the Claddagh rolls down to
the sea…

It was her gift to me and it made me so happy,

With this on my finger my heart it would sing;

No king on his throne could be half so happy

As I am when I'm wearing my old Claddagh
ring.

Introduction

Whether you were given a Claddagh ring by your grandmother, used it to represent your eternal love for your beloved other half, or just have simply seen this distinctive ring and wondered where it came from, I hope this book will speak to you.

There are so many questions one could ask about the Claddagh ring. Where exactly did it come from? What is its history? Why has it become an emblem of Ireland almost on the same level as St. Patrick, the Irish flag, or the shamrock? Why has its symbolism captured the hearts of so many? How and when did it become popular internationally? From a monarch to a fisherman's wife, countless people have worn this ring with pleasure and pride.

In this little book that I hope you'll cherish, I've set out to explore the folklore, myths, and historical origins of this distinctive piece of Irish jewelry. I'll discuss the traditions attached to it, the people who wore it and what it meant to them in their everyday lives.

Love and friendship, crowned by loyalty. Those three powerful elements sum up the importance of the ring worn by millions of Irish and others over the past few centuries. Even if you haven't owned one, chances are you've seen someone wearing one or seen an image of it someplace. Yet, even with the Claddagh ring's fame, very few people know the history of where it came from or how it became so popular worldwide.

I'll tell you about the small Galway fishing village that gave the ring its name. The Claddagh is a unique place, with its own fascinating traditions even beyond the Claddagh ring. It's a community that can teach us much about Irish history and culture. The Claddagh people's proud yet gentle ways and their charming cottages intrigued travelers in the 19th and 20th centuries. I'll share some of those first-hand accounts of their impressions as they observed a fishing community who held on to an age-old way of life, directly in the shadow of a prosperous walled city full of foreign influences.

Nowadays, there are pubs bearing the name of Claddagh from the US to the UK. There's even a healthcare center in Massachusetts with the name. 'Claddagh' has become a symbol of Irishness across the globe. Still, don't think that the Claddagh ring appeals only to those of Irish heritage. There are many of all nationalities who feel drawn to the ring's story of love, friendship and loyalty, and admire its distinctive look. So, without further ado, let's go on the journey of the Claddagh ring.

Let love and friendship reign!

Chapter One

The Ancestors
of the Claddagh Ring

The Claddagh ring's design features have ancient precedents. The ring's unique combination of elements was influenced by European fede rings. The name *fede* comes from the Italian phrase "mani in fede," which means "hands in faith." These rings date back to ancient Roman times. Such jewelry was a widespread token of betrothal in medieval Europe and eventually influenced the design of the Claddagh ring. Fede rings might not have been common in the Emerald Isle but Ireland did have an extensive trade with the European mainland and overseas fashions and ideas definitely had an influence on Irish culture and customs.

During the medieval and then the Renaissance periods, various regional variants of the fede rings emerged. The Claddagh ring uses the fede design's clasped hands but adds a heart (symbolizing love) and a crown (indicating loyalty). While the fede and Claddagh rings have a common ancestor, the addition of the heart and crown give the Claddagh its distinct iconic identity. Similar designs were definitely in circulation in the northern French province of Brittany and there was significant trade between Galway and St. Malo, the main port of Brittany. For instance, Irish state papers in 1548 note "The arrival of a big ship at Kinsale from St. Malo, going to Galway with wine to take fifteen lasts of hides from there." However, none of these other designs has stood the test of time or become as widespread as the distinctive Claddagh design. Nor did they become as representative of a culture as the Claddagh ring has become of Ireland. Only the Claddagh ring that has become recognized and beloved the world over.

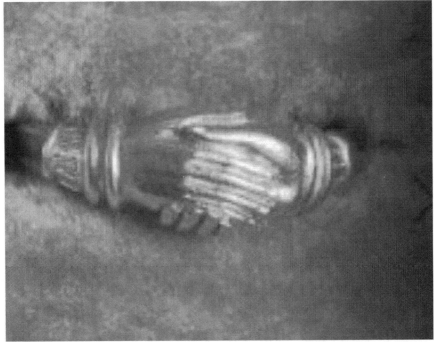

Illustration of a Medieval 'Fede' Ring, Ancestor of The Claddagh Ring

Chapter Two

The Meaning of
The Heart, Hands, and Crown

The Claddagh ring, with its fascinating design of a heart grasped by two hands and capped with a crown, is more than just a piece of jewelry—it's a testimony to what constitutes true love. The heart, hands, and crown each express a meaningful message that resonates powerfully with those familiar with its lore. These symbols reflect three timeless characteristics that serve as the cornerstone of genuine human relationships: love, friendship, and loyalty. These three qualities are created in the fires of struggle and are as tough as steel. A relationship where friendship, love, and loyalty prevail does not simply happen; it is built one day at a time.

The Claddagh is a subset of the much larger ring category known as *fede,* or faith rings. As mentioned earlier, fede is an abbreviation of the Italian phrase *mani in fede,* which translates as 'hands united in faithfulness.' These were regarded as physical representations of friendship or love, similar to modern wedding rings. Before the passing of Lord Hardwicke's Marriage Act of 1753, marriage was governed by the local traditions and customs. A marriage ceremony could be as simple as joining hands and might or might not involve the exchange of rings. Marriage ceremonies among ordinary people were simple affairs and therefore a ring such as a Claddagh ring would take on incredible significance as something very special. Sometimes bride and groom wouldn't even have worn special clothes for their wedding, only their Sunday best, and the reception would have been a simple meal.

The Heart:

The heart, an age-old symbol of love, is at the center of the Claddagh design. This internationally recognizable emblem represents the seat of emotion and passion in a multitude of cultures and eras. The heart holds a special significance in the context of the Claddagh ring. It represents the strong affection and warmth that connects two individuals, whether in romance, family, or a close-knit friendship. When given as a gift, the Claddagh ring's heart serves as a proclamation of devotion. It might be a passionate pledge spoken by romantic lovers or an expression of familial love shared by a parent and child. 'Macree' (or *mo chroí* in the original Gaelic) was a fond term of endearment, as in the 1910 American-Irish song, "Mother Macree," when it was used to designate the lasting love a child has for its mother. Because of the many varieties of love, the Claddagh ring is versatile and plays a vital role in many different types of relationships.

The Hands:

The two hands cradling the heart represent friendship, trust, and unity. Hands are, by definition, a means to make connections. They enable us to reach out, touch, hold, and support others. Holding hands symbolizes solidarity, support, and friendship in all cultures. It's no wonder, then, that the hands play an important role in the Claddagh ring's design, supporting the heart and emphasizing the idea that true love flourishes on the foundation of true friendship. The hands may also symbolize 'helping hands' and a willingness to be there in times of trouble. Of course, the hands also symbolize joining together two souls on a lifelong journey, as evidenced by the tradition of 'handfasting,' or joining together hands in a ritual to make a relationship permanent. In ancient Ireland, dating back long beyond 7000 B.C., two persons who chose to marry were brought together, frequently on a feast day such as Beltane, the Celtic Mayday festival. The couple faced each other, holding each other's hands with their arms extended while a braided cord was fastened around their hands. The Druid priest would then declare that by this joining of hands the two people were now united.

The Claddagh ring honors not only romantic love but also the platonic connections that enrich our lives, reminding wearers that romantic love is as much about being the closest of friends as it is about being romantic partners.

The Crown:

A royal crown sits atop the heart, indicating loyalty, a virtue that prevails in every lasting relationship. The crown represents the pledge of honor and devotion someone makes to their beloved. Loyalty is the everlasting dedication that sees partnerships through the hard times as well as the days of romance. The Claddagh ring's crown serves as a reminder of one's duty to be truthful, steadfast, and devoted in a partnership. The high position of the crown over the heart suggests that love and friendship, however profound, require the protecting and honoring mantle of commitment in order to truly thrive.

The Whole Picture:

Together, the three elements of a Claddagh ring present a complete picture of a true relationship. With its gracefully intertwined emblems of the heart, hands, and crown, it conveys to wearers and to the world at large that love is most profound when it is nurtured by the hands of kindness and honored with the dignity of loyalty. The Claddagh ring's eternal message of love, friendship, and commitment has made it a cherished token for all ages and across nations. Whether worn as a sign of romantic commitment, a symbol of friendship, or a treasure to be passed down through generations, this unique ring is a touching tribute to the eternal essence of human connection.

There are those who also see a spiritual dimension to the meaning of the Claddagh ring. Like the shamrock, another symbol of Ireland, its three elements could represent the Christian view of God, with the Trinity of Father, Son, and the Holy Spirit. Although perhaps not the most common interpretation, it shows that the more we ponder the meaning of the Claddagh ring, its origins and its legends, the more insights and inspiration we can gain from this intriguing piece of jewelry.

Chapter Three

How To Wear It

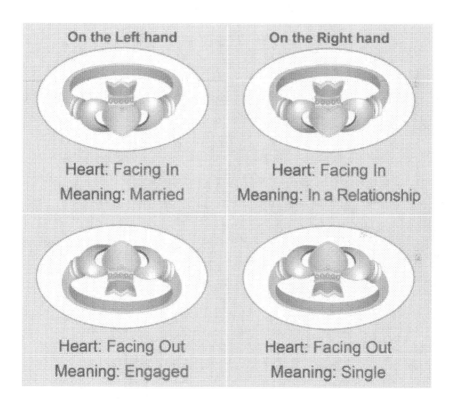

The meaning of the Claddagh ring goes beyond its design. Long before a status on your Facebook page indicated whether you were married, single or 'it's complicated,' the Claddagh ring was conveying that message to the world. Which hand you wear the ring on has a special significance. Which direction the heart is facing is also crucial to its meaning for you and what you communicate about your relationship status to the world.

+ If you wear it on your right hand with the heart pointing outward in the direction of the fingertips, you're single and could be in search of love.

+ If you wear it on your right hand with the heart pointing inward toward your heart, you are in a relationship and your heart is spoken for.

+ If you wear it on the ring finger of your left hand with the point of the heart facing outward toward your fingertips, then you are engaged.

+ If you wear it on the ring finger of your left hand with the point of the heart facing inward towards your heart, you are married.

Chapter Four

The Origins of The Claddagh Ring

**Illustration Of Claddagh Ring From 1840 Book,
"Tour of Ireland," Mr & Mrs. Hall**

Many people of Irish descent, both men and women, frequently don the Claddagh as a symbol of their deep connection and dedication to their Irish heritage. In a 1906 article in the *Journal of the Galway Archaeological and Historical Society* titled, "The Claddagh Ring," Galway jeweler William Dillon noted the Claddagh tradition spanned "roughly from the Aran Isles on the West, all through Connemara and Joyce's Country and then eastwards and southwards for not more than 12 miles." Traditionally, the people of this area referred to it as the 'heart and hands' ring. The term 'Claddagh ring' became widely recognized only in the mid-19th century. Its naming can be linked to an Irish travel narrative published in London during the 1840s, in which authors Mr. and Mrs. Samuel Carter Hall described the Claddagh community, stating, "They have many peculiar customs. One is worthy of special note. The wedding ring is an heirloom in the family. It is regularly transferred (by a mother) to her daughter. These rings are largely of solid gold and not infrequently cost from two to three pounds each."

As Ida Delamar points out in her scrupulously researched 1996 article in the *Irish Arts Review*, the earliest surviving Irish rings of the Claddagh design that we know of date from the early 1700s. One was made by a Galway goldsmith, Richard Joyce, but the other three are stamped with the mark of Thomas Meade, a goldsmith from the County Cork town of Kinsale - like Galway, a seaport.

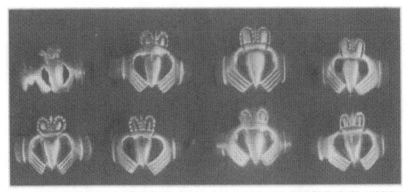

6. CLADDAGH RINGS: The Hon. Garech Browne's Collection. This collection which was originally made between c. 1910 and 1940 by John Costelloe of Tuam includes the earliest known Claddagh ring (top left) which was made by Richard Joyce of Galway (see Fig. 2).

**Some of the Oldest Claddagh Rings
In Existence. Source: Collection Of the Hon. Garech Browne**

There are various theories about what might have happened to any Claddagh rings before those that have survived to the present day. Some suppose that older rings could have been sold in the hundreds, as desperate inhabitants of the area around Galway wanted to pay their way to America to escape the hunger and economic collapse in Ireland that came in the wake of the 1847 Irish potato famine. Because so many of these rings flooded the market and an impoverished populace had no means or desire to acquire them, it's believed they were melted down for the value of the gold. Another (not necessarily contradictory) theory holds that earlier rings may have been made of less expensive metals, and when people could afford gold ones—and wanted the status and economic security that a gold ring could bring—these earlier rings were abandoned. This hypothesis is supported by William Dillon in his 1906 article in the *Journal of the Galway Archaeological and Historical Society*, because he alludes to a bronze Claddagh ring being found in late 19th century excavations that was clearly made from an ordinary coin.

There are also accounts of French rings similar to the Claddagh ring found in the northern coastal province of Brittany, where they were popular among sailors. Given Galway's centuries-long status as a port trading with the European continent, could some foreign sailors have brought the ring to Galway, where it was admired, copied and generally adopted by the people of the Claddagh? Could this also explain why early examples of the Claddagh ring design were made by a goldsmith from Kinsale, another seaport that would have traded with the European continent? It seems a plausible explanation. Rings are passed along, inherited or sold. Sometimes, they remain hidden for centuries. Perhaps in years to come, some will come up for auction, or be recovered from the back of a drawer in a museum and will prove to be "the missing link." Or, a learned scholar may find a description in a long-lost letter between medieval sweethearts discussing the ring that is the symbol of their love, a mention that will provide further insight into the origins of the Claddagh ring.

Although its precise origins are obscure, this ring was embraced wholeheartedly by the people of the Claddagh, bestowed with the Claddagh name, and from that point on became known across the world as the Claddagh ring, or *fáinne an Chladaigh*, a symbol of Irish heritage. William Dillon's 1906 article notes that he was impressed by the willingness of the people of the Claddagh to spend large sums of money on the rings, much more than people of surrounding areas. The ring had strong emotional power for them and they were willing to make great sacrifices to own one, passing them on to their family as treasured heirlooms.

This then poses the question, why did the ring not remain solely among the people of the Claddagh? To answer this, we need to examine the unique nature of the Claddagh, a fishing village so unique and fascinating that it was well documented by visitors to Ireland in books they wrote about their travels, to such a point that the Claddagh was recommended as a must-see for travelers of that era. These tales of traditional Irish culture were fascinating and would have provided a romantic association for the ring, setting the foundation for its wide embrace by people across the world either deeply attached to their own Irish heritage and seeking a token of it, or by those of any heritage who loved both the ring's symbolism and the fact that it came from a place and time shrouded in a bit of mystery. Furthermore, due to poor economic prospects in Ireland, many Claddagh people were forced to emigrate and would have taken the tradition of the Claddagh ring with them around the globe.

1906 Advertisement for Dillon's Claddagh Rings

The late 19th century was the time of the Gaelic revival, a movement to revive the Irish language and to preserve other elements of Irish culture, such as poetry and music. The interest in Ireland's ancient culture, its traditions and any artifacts that offered insight into Ireland's past was widespread. Ireland's legends were revived, songs were written and Irish artifacts were much sought after. Not coincidentally, this was when the Tara brooch, an 8th-century piece, was found on a beach in County Meath in the East of Ireland. It's hardly surprising then to see an advertisement like the one I have shared here, in which Dillon's jewelers proudly offer not just rings, but brooches, bracelets, earrings, cufflinks and other jewelry. Noteworthy in this advertisement is the reference to a host of British aristocracy and royalty, an aspirational nod to the rich and powerful of the day. It's also worth noting that Queen Victoria (probably seeking to legitimize the British empire's control of Ireland) wore a Claddagh ring and even gave one as a gift to her son, Edward VII.

Chapter Five

The Claddagh Ring's Legendary Legacy

What would a book about Ireland and Irish culture be without legends? Indeed, there are two particularly interesting tales relating to the origins of the Claddagh ring. One of them is rather fanciful and enchanting, involving messengers from the animal world. The other is hard to authenticate in all its details but could quite likely be true. The two legends involve sea voyages and heartache, classical elements for many a romantic tale. Both of them relate to the Joyce family. An understanding of who the Joyce family was provides interesting context for the stories. Firstly, Galway in medieval times was like a city-state with tight rules on commerce, taxes, and law and order, including who could enter or live within the city walls. The 14 clans who ruled the city were known as the 'Tribes of Galway.' They were Athy, Blake, Bodkin, Browne, D'arcy, Deane, Font, Ffrench, Joyce, Kirwan, Lynch, Martin, Morris and Skerrett.

The Joyce family stands as one of Galway's renowned tribes, lending their name to a region in Connemara, known as Joyce Country. This region, set against the backdrop of mountains, straddles the boundary between northern Galway and southern Mayo. Originating from the Flemish fore-name 'Jos', the Joyce surname in Ireland is quite distinctive. This family established a presence in Ireland during the Norman invasion of the medieval era. By the late 1200s, the pioneering Joyces had made their home in the northwest region of Connacht. Over time, they journeyed southwards to Galway, assimilating with the locals, particularly through intermarriage. Their most significant association was with the O'Flaherty clan, famed sea marauders of the aforementioned Connemara. As Normans who integrated deeply with native Irish culture, the Joyces found themselves in a unique position, straddling two worlds. This perhaps explains their scant mention in both Irish chronicles and Dublin's colonial archives. Their inaugural appearance in Irish historical records was in 1560, where Joyce Country was highlighted as the entry point to West Connacht.

Despite the tumultuous periods between the 1580s and 1690s, when Ireland faced three consecutive conquests, the Joyce legacy persisted in Galway. They flourished as merchants, traders, and esteemed townsmen. With the discovery of the Americas in 1492, Galway's importance grew, serving as the final European stop on trans-Atlantic journeys. Through all these shifts, the Joyce family remained an integral part of Galway's fabric. Each of the legends has as its background a Joyce involved with overseas travel and exotic encounters far away from Galway.

Legend One: The Brave and Romantic Mr. Joyce

In the late 17th century, an intrepid young man from the west of Ireland, Richard Joyce, set out on a journey from Galway to the West Indies. Alas, he never arrived at this destination, as his ship was captured by North African pirates. Young Joyce was transported to Algiers, where he was enslaved and sold to a wealthy goldsmith. The goldsmith noticed immediately that Joyce was intelligent and trained him in the trade of goldsmithing. Richard spent almost 15 years working for his master in Algeria, all the while pining for a sweetheart he had left behind in Galway. Some sources say he invented the Claddagh ring while thinking of his faraway love, to represent his eternal love, longed-for companionship with her, and above all, his loyalty to her in his many years of exile.

Because of its similarities to previous Egyptian rings, others wonder if he copied or adapted a design he'd seen while in Algiers. We'll never know. However, there is one verifiable historic fact, which is that in 1689, King William III issued an order that all his subjects (which at that time included the Irish) who were enslaved were to be set free, and the North African ruler complied. As a result of this order, Joyce was at long last free. But the goldsmith was impressed by Joyce's skills and character and had become quite fond of the young Irishman. He was very unhappy at the prospect of Joyce leaving, so to entice him to remain in Algiers, the goldsmith offered Richard his beautiful daughter in marriage and half the goldsmithing business. However, Joyce refused and returned home. There he was apparently reunited with the lovely Galway girl he had left behind. She had never considered another suitor for even a moment and had been waiting for him through the many years of his captivity.

Joyce proceeded to establish himself as a goldsmith in Galway. The first Claddagh rings that can be identified bore his symbol, as well as the first initials of his name, R.I. (Richard Ioyes--a variation of Richard Joyce). [NOTE: at this time, people often substituted an I for a J on signatures and in normal writing.] Joyce's goldsmith business thrived and he was able to set himself up in style, with a country estate a couple of miles outside Galway in the area of Rahoon. Joyce's silver creations, which can be identified by his stamp and initials, are still in existence today. Among these are chalices and sacred church silverware inscribed with the initials R.I. and an anchor signifying hope. No antique Claddagh rings carrying Joyce's name have been discovered, probably because they wore out or were melted down to sell during difficult financial times. Still, Joyce is thought by many to be the brains behind the Claddagh ring.

Another legend, however, holds that the distinctive design was created by his relative, Margaret of the Bridges, an inspiring and intrepid lady whose tale we'll delve into on the following pages.

Legend Two: The Beautiful and Charitable Margaret

A charming legend regarding the Claddagh ring comes from the life of one Margaret Joyce, also known as "Margaret of the Bridges." The details of her tale vary depending on which source you consult, but it's said that she caught the eye of a Spanish merchant visiting Galway, when he noticed her washing laundry in a stream. This detail seems rather unlikely, though, as Margaret was a member of a prosperous Galway family. Regardless, the Spanish merchant somehow made her acquaintance and fell madly in love with her. He, and presumably also his large fortune, was attractive to her and she agreed to marry and live in Spain with him. However, the romantic Spaniard with an eye for the Irish lady was quite a few years her senior and died before long, leaving her his vast fortune.

Poor Margaret packed up her belongings and returned to her native Galway. Once home, she didn't let grief overcome her or luxurious idleness distract her. She set about building bridges all around the western province of Connaught, of which Galway would be considered the capital city. These bridges would have connected remote areas with centers of commerce and brought prosperity to the countryside. Still a young woman, Margaret remarried in 1596, choosing as her husband Oliver Og French, the mayor of Galway. Due to his responsibilities as a merchant prince of Galway, which was an international trading post, he would embark on overseas voyages. While he was away on one such journey, Margaret was sitting down while supervising the building of a bridge, when lo and behold, an eagle flew overhead and dropped a gold ring in her lap! This was presumably a reward for her good works and charity, but maybe also a tribute to her willingness to take a chance on love.

It is said that this form of the ring may have been the original design of the Claddagh ring. There are accounts in the family papers of various prominent Galway families descended from Margaret that tell of exceptionally fine jewels inherited from her. One of these may have been the Claddagh ring dropped in her lap from the heavens. Or, her original Claddagh ring could have inspired descendants to create similar rings. Such a design may have been known to Richard Joyce, one of those descendants who lived in the century after Margaret and, as we've just read, practiced as a goldsmith and is credited with the creation of some of the earliest Claddagh rings.

Chapter Six

Where Is 'The Claddagh'?

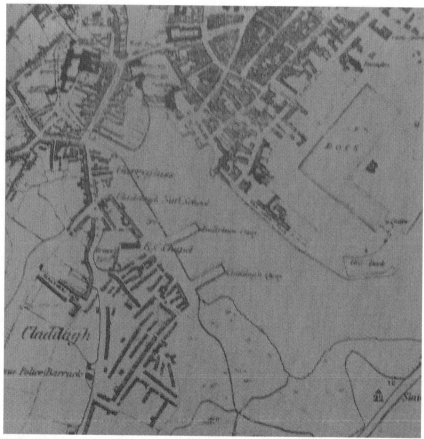

ORDNANCE SURVEY MAP, 1838-1840 (CLADDAGH ON THE LEFT,
GALWAY CITY ON THE RIGHT)

Although many people have heard of the Claddagh ring, few know much about the place called the Claddagh. Pronounced 'kladda' and deriving from the Irish Gaelic for a rocky shore or stony beach, the Claddagh is located where the river Corrib flows into Galway Bay. The Claddagh was always a fishing village, almost certainly the oldest such community in Ireland. The settlement's roots may go back to the Stone Age, if we use accounts of ancient tools found there as a guide. It seems always to have been a peaceful place, as no weapons or evidence of fortifications have ever been found there. Its existence predates that of the city of Galway.

The earliest recorded reference to the area of the Claddagh comes from the recollections of St. Enda who lived in the 5th century. He describes meeting a boy who came from a harbor who presented him with a fish, indicating both the importance of fishing to the local economy even back then and the innate generosity of the Claddagh people. In the 12th and 13th centuries, the Claddagh people would have seen a succession of forts belonging to Irish tribes on the opposite side of the river gradually be replaced by a stone castle built by the Norman leader Richard de Burgo, who banished the Gaelic O'Flahertys across the Corrib. The castle came under attack from the native Irish and this led to more fortifications and eventually a walled city. An inscription was placed above the West Gate of the town that declared, "From the ferocious O'Flaherties, Good Lord, deliver us."

As H.V. Morton explains in his 1930 book, *In Search of Ireland*, Galway became "a kind of city-state ruled over by ruling families called 'the tribes,' 14 clans in total: Athy, Blake, Bodkin, Browne, D'Arcy, Deane, Font, Ffrench, Joyce, Kirwan, Lynch, Martin, Morris and Skerrett." Galway's port traded in items ranging from wine to amber with the cities of continental Europe and was a stopping-off point for those en route to the Americas. Columbus is said to have stopped there on his voyage of discovery. The ruling Norman families of Galway were wary of the native Irish and enforced laws regarding their presence inside the walls. Yet the Irish settlement of the Claddagh remained just across the river from the old medieval walls of Galway city.

The Claddagh was inhabited by fishermen whose wives sold their catch near the Spanish Arch, a portal in the walls of Galway. The community maintained its separate status from outsiders. Eyewitness accounts tell us that even in the late 19th century, visitors to the community had to announce their business and have it approved before they could cross the bridge from the city and enter the village. English was the principal language within the walls of Galway city, but the Claddagh on the other side of the river remained a Gaelic-speaking outpost until into the 20th century. In 1808, the fisherman gathered money to pave the village with cobblestones. These people didn't marry outsiders and maintained a set of traditions distinct from others near them. Observers remarked how its customs and traditions set it apart from other places on the outskirts of Galway like Woodquay and Bohermore on the other side of the city. While in 1695, it had 528 inhabitants, by 1812, the population of the Claddagh had grown to almost 3,000, with over 2,000 of them fishermen.

In Henry D. Inglis's book, *Ireland in 1834,* he remarks that the people "seldom leave the Claddagh, unless merely to take their fish to market; hold no intercourse with townspeople; and marry entirely among each other." Their housing consisted of whitewashed thatched cottages set in 'clachans' or irregular groupings of houses set at angles to each other. Although humble, people took pride in their houses, keeping them neat and tidy. As H.V. Morton remarks in *In Search of Ireland,* "Through open doors you see little rooms with low ceilings. These are warm, clean and comfortable; but so small… and in these rooms, warm with the peat fires and loud with crickets piping in the ashes, a red light is burning before the Sacred Heart [Author's Noe: The Sacred Heart was a picture of Jesus that was very commonly displayed in Irish homes over the fireplace]."

Other visitors commented on the kitchen dressers, the large cabinets that proudly displayed an array of gleaming dishes, glassware, and shining mugs hanging by handles, ready for everyday use. The more ornamental and fancier plates were mainly for display and for use when 'visitors' came calling. This fishing village charmed visitors. Morton described it thus: "Nothing is more picturesque…If you took three hundred little toy cottages, and jumbled them up on a nursery floor you would have something like the Claddagh. It is a triumph of unconscious beauty."

SILVER ALBUMEN PRINT OF THE CLADDAGH, APPROX. 1860

The Claddagh, Co. Galway city, 1901

Chapter Seven

Fishing

Photograph Of Galway Hooker, By Maura Mullarkey, 2023

S ituated as it was on Galway Bay, with its ample amounts of herring, cod and haddock, the Claddagh's location made fishing the main economic activity. However, unlike in other fishing communities, fishing and related activities were the exclusive occupation practiced by the inhabitants. In fact, a Galway city corporation bylaw of 1585 recognized the importance of fishing to the area's sustenance and commerce by forbidding fishermen from using a spade or plough, activities that might "barr them from fyshing." The importance of the sale of fish to Galway's economy is evidenced in the royal charter of 1351, asserting the city's right to collect taxes on the fish brought into the city, "for every measure of herring, a farthing." The fisherfolk of the Claddagh claimed the whole bay as their own to fish and for others to venture out into those waters left open the possibility of swift retribution by having their boats destroyed.

By the mid-19th century, the Claddagh was home to the largest fishing fleet in Ireland. Herring was the main catch. At the height of fishing activity, there were approximately 150 sailboats and more than 100 rowing boats. When it comes to sea-going craft, there was a wide array, including smaller boats known by evocative Irish names such as the Leathbhád, Gleoiteog and Púcán. However, it is the Galway Hooker (or 'an bád mór'- large boat in Irish) that is most associated with the Claddagh and has been revived in recent times as a vehicle of heritage and leisure rather than serious commercial enterprise. With its black hull, coated in a mixture of creosote and coal. and three red sails, its angular silhouette and starkly contrasting colors make it instantly recognizable. Author Mary Banim describes them in 1892 as seeming "to ride on the waves with the ease and buoyancy of a bird."

Another feature of the Claddagh fishermen much remarked upon by outside observers was their complex system of designating when it was unlucky or unsuitable to go to sea, which meant they often missed out on large quantities of fish, even when they may have dearly needed the income. When not at sea, the men occupied themselves with keeping their boats and fishing equipment at the ready, making repairs to hulls, sails and nets. Their wives and children pitched in by gathering bait (either worms or mussels) and placing these on the long fishing lines that would be dragged through the sea to snag the fish. The wife of the Claddagh King, Mrs. Padge King, noted in 1892 of the good years, "What the bank is to the landsfolk the sea was to the fisherman. He had only to cast his nets an' draw more fish than he wanted, for then the bay swarmed with every fish."

Unfortunately, those good years became more and more infrequent as time marched on. Before the arrival of large steam trawlers, fishing provided for the community's needs. At the end of the fishing season, the boats were used for bringing peat turf as fuel from Connemara to the people of Galway town and its surroundings. Some boats were used to transport seaweed from the shore to sell it to inland farmers along the river Corrib for use as fertilizer on their fields.

GIRL OF THE CLADDAGH, DRAWING, 1855

**THE BLESSING OF THE BAY, SKETCH AUTHOR'S OWN,
INSPIRED BY VINTAGE PRINT**

Chapter Eight

The Claddagh People –
A Law unto Themselves

Street vendors, The Quays, Galway city, 1902

An account that appeared in the *Ulster Journal of Archaeology* in 1854 gives us quite a few specifics about the lives of the people in the Claddagh in the 19th century. The writer begins by describing the people there as "purely Irish, of the most ancient Celtic type" and notes nearly all having typically Irish surnames, including Connolly, O'Flaherty, Murphy, O'Halloran, Tierney, Rainey, and O'Brien. The first names are typical of those found in Ireland at the time, with many Johns, Michaels, Patricks, and a host of Marys and Catherines. The writer notes that there are so many men of the same first name that to distinguish among them, the men are given nicknames based on various types of fish. For example, there'd be a 'Jack the hake' or 'Joe the trout' and so on. Over 50 years later, in Stephen Gwynn's 1909 *A Holiday in Connemara*, the author notes that the town has "remained Irish," by which he meant the dress and customs of an older Ireland had been maintained. He describes women who are bare-footed with their shawls and petticoats typical of the countryside further away from Galway city.

Yet despite having many traditions typical of Connemara, outsiders either from the Galway countryside or the city didn't make their homes among the people of the Claddagh. The patron saint of the area was St. Nicholas, a generous man who was the model for Santa Claus (a corruption of Saint Nick-laus), an early Christian bishop venerated by many diverse groups, including merchants, archers, repentant thieves, but most pertinent to the Claddagh, by sailors. Among the powers attributed to him was the calming of storms at sea, an attribute no doubt highly valued by the fishing community of the Claddagh. Life revolved around fishing and traditions were carefully maintained.

One of the defining features of the community was its leadership by the King of The Claddagh. This was an elected position but the king's word was binding when it came to disputes and to all matters related to the whys and wherefores of fishing. The community was known as an orderly place, with theft virtually unknown and homes notable for their lack of locks or bolts. The primary distinction between the Claddagh village and the developing contemporary Ireland of the 1800s lay in the village's progressive gender roles—women were in charge of not only unloading the fish from the boats but also managing their sale.

THE MEN OF THE CLADDAGH

**TWO CLADDAGH FISHERMEN, 19th CENTURY, SKETCH
AUTHOR'S OWN, INSPIRED BY VINTAGE PHOTOGRAPH**

The sole occupation of the men of the Claddagh was fishing, and as young men they spent much time acquiring the skills that were to last them a lifetime. They were inward-looking, content to socialize among other members of the community. Some writers claimed they rarely took interest in politics, even at times when most Irish people would have been actively engaged in Nationalist activity. It seemed they had little interest in land rights, the breaking up of old Anglo-Irish estates or Irish independence. Their world was and always had been focused on their fishing activities and their traditions. They were not belligerent as a whole and an excerpt from *The Ulster Journal of Archaeology* of 1854 notes "They are not boxers" but "touch one and you hurt them all." The writer goes on to say that "There are no braver men at sea than the Claddagh fisherman." There are many accounts of how these men bravely withstood storms and accidents, fiercely battling on to beat back the might of an unforgiving sea. Their perspective was fixed on the sea and all matters related to securing a respectable catch.

The selling of the fish and all commercial matters related to that were left solely in the charge of the women. The men were also noteworthy for the gentle care they took of young children while the women were tending to the house or out selling the catch that had just been brought ashore. As Stephen Gwynn put it, "In at least a dozen houses, I found the woman bustling about while the man sat or stood with an infant on his arm - and holding it as a woman does." These men were indeed quite different to other men of their time. When finances allowed, they splashed on their Sunday best, as James Hardiman remarked in *The History of the Town and County of the Town of Galway*, their formal dress including "a pair of new brogues, a broad trimmed hat neither cocked nor slouched, and a red silk handkerchief about [his] neck."

THE WOMEN OF THE CLADDAGH

Galway shawl on fish seller, Claddagh,

The Claddagh women were a resilient and enterprising lot. They would keep the households going while their husbands were out at sea, with visitors to the Claddagh remarking on the neatness and obvious pride taken in their homes. When the fishing fleet came home, the women went down to unload the boats. Once the fish came ashore, the women were in sole charge of everything to do with their storage and sale, while older women and menfolk would look after children and keep the household running smoothly. Dressed in their distinctive shawls that sheltered them from the rain and the cold, the women would cross the bridge to sell the catch at an open area in front of the Spanish Arch (the last remnant of Galway city's medieval walls). This flat selling place upon which the fish were spread was known as 'the concrete.' Here the women would get the attention of potential customers with a joke or funny observation. Their quick wit was often remarked upon and, like salespeople of any ilk, an outgoing nature and ability to interact with others in an engaging manner was essential. As fish are obviously perishable, they would have to have possessed a keen sense of when they could press for a higher price and when a lower price for a quick sale would be more advantageous. Their family's survival depended on an acute awareness of making as much profit as possible.

When at the market, the women's 'praíscín,' or rough canvas apron, was both a place to store smaller merchandise like prawns and a change purse or shopkeeper's till. Not only were the Claddagh women responsible for unloading the fish and getting it to market, they were responsible for securing bait like worms and mussels from the shoreline and baiting the hook. More importantly, and more unusual for the time, they also were solely responsible for how the household's finances were managed, being completely in charge of all major expenditures, savings and whatever modest amount might have remained for discretionary spending. It was the ladies who decided what the menfolk would be allocated for alcohol and tobacco. The women made sure they also had a share of life's indulgent vices, as Hardiman recounts, when referring to whiskey, brandy and tobacco, "of which they themselves also liberally partake."

The men were masters of their domain at sea, being brave and skilled at the ways of the fish and the sea's potential for danger. However, as Mary Banim's 1892 *Here and There Through Ireland* explains, the finances are left to the women as they consider that their men "are not sufficiently accustomed to the cunning twists and turns of the sharks that inhabit land… and so the women it is who manage all affairs connected with life on land, and who are universally considered more quick-witted and more acutely intelligent than their husbands and brothers." When the women's children were reared and the cut and thrust of unloading and selling the days' catches became too much for them as they became older, they were in charge of the younger children while the men were fishing or mending their nets and boats and the younger women, the bean an tí (woman of the house), ran their fish-selling enterprises.

In an interesting nod to the prevalence of the Irish language in the Claddagh, women who could not speak English did not wear ribbons in their caps. The traditional female dress of the Claddagh was described by Mary Banim as "white cap, without a riband - the sign before now of one who spoke only Irish - a blue nap cloak, of the form peculiar to the women of the Claddagh and of Connemara, a red kerchief on the head, a plain gown tucked up over a crimson petticoat, and save on Sundays and holidays - the bare feet." Going barefoot was not only an economy but also was considered healthier for the women, as had they worn shoes and socks, these would have been almost always damp. At least when they were barefoot their feet would have a chance to dry. It wasn't until the 20th century that the more traditional dress became relegated to every day, with Sunday best becoming a means to keep up in a modest way with the changing fashions of Galway's smart set, who would have looked to Dublin, London, and Paris for their inspiration. However, even as the fashions changed and the old traditional garb was discarded, the women clung fast to their tradition of wearing the Claddagh ring and passing these heirlooms down through their families.

COURTSHIP AND MARRIAGE CUSTOMS IN THE CLADDAGH

Marriage in the Claddagh was traditionally within the community. Courtship was closely linked to the calendar of traditional feast days. St. Patrick's Day, fair days and especially midsummer eve were opportunities for young lads to focus their attentions (and intentions) on the young ladies who caught their fancy. Feast days were usually accompanied by the lighting of bonfires. A young man would grab a lighted stick from the flames and throw it in the direction of the object of his desires. If interested in his advances, she would throw it back toward him. Once the couple were betrothed, attention turned to securing a Claddagh ring. This represented a huge expenditure for the Claddagh people and, after a share in a fishing boat, would have been their most substantial asset. The ring's symbolism of love, friendship and loyalty resonated deeply with the tightly knit community whose bonds weathered good times and bad.

This gift was far more than a simple exchange; it was a sincere act brimming with sentiment and romance. When the woman accepted the ring, she would place it on her right hand with the heart's point directed outward to her fingertips, indicating to all that her heart was promised to another. This served as a visible declaration of their mutual devotion and their forthcoming marriage. Upon her wedding, she would place it on the ring finger of her left hand, rotating the ring to point the tip of the heart inward towards her wrist, in the direction of her own heart. The ring became the property of the women and was passed down through the generations. Strangely, though, some accounts note that many of the oldest rings were sized for men, so perhaps the tradition of inheritance in the female line doesn't stretch back that far in history. However, many of these treasured emblems of romantic love and family tradition were dispersed to all parts of the world when the inhabitants emigrated. Others were pawned and later melted down, in what must have been an occasion of heartbreak for their owners.

THE KING OF THE CLADDAGH

SKETCH OF PADNEEN KING, THE KING OF THE CLADDAGH (WITH HIS WIFE & SON) 1865

One of the most notable features of the Claddagh was that it was ruled over by a king who was elected annually and chosen for his knowledge, honesty and impartiality. As Mary Banim puts it in her book, "Unlike all other sovereigns, the Claddagh king, while supreme in [his] authority, never tried to take any worldly advantage over his fellows; he was always, as now, a fisherman as humble as, and no richer than, the others." *The Illustrated London News* tells us in 1870 that the Claddagh people "elect a sort of mayor, who was styled the King of the Claddagh, and as a mark of distinction had the privilege of flying a white flag on the mast of his fishing boat, and who moreover, had the power of deciding all disputes that might arise within the community in a most absolute manner.' In an

1880 edition of the same publication, we learn of the ceremony surrounding the appointment of the new king, which tells us that the monarch was yearly chosen by "The Claddagh Boys on the eve of St. John [Author's note - 23ʳᵈ of June]. A procession of men and women, bearing long faces of dock-stems, escort him through the quarter, and when proclamation has been duly made, bonfires are lighted in honour of his reign for the ensuing twelve months. His ensign is a white flag, and he is empowered to decide all quarrels and punish all minor offences among the Claddagh population, without troubling the police and legal magistracy at all."

As well as matters on land, the king took on the responsibilities of an admiral, leading the fishing fleet, with his sail being a distinctive white while the others were red. He decided which days the fleet would set sail. Once at sea, Mary Banim tells us that he "chose the fishing ground and gave the signal, at which every boat cast its nets at the same moment, so that all might be equal sharers in the harvest God was pleased to send." Although considerate and fair when giving all the Claddagh fishermen a chance, the king also could be fierce in defending the Claddagh fishing grounds from outsiders, as any outsider found fishing in their patch was liable to have his net and boat destroyed.

Although the Claddagh kings dated back centuries, there was no central record of who was elected in which year. The first newspaper mention of a specific king is found in *The Galway Vindicator* of May 1887, in an article paying tribute to the then most recent king, the priest of the parish, the Very Reverend Father Folan, who they reported "for many years before his lamentable death, was regularly elected as King." However, at one stage around 1892, from Mary Banim we learn that the "custom of appointing their own ruler prevails among the Claddagh folk at the present day, with the difference that, in place of an annual election, the distinction seems to have become vested in one family, whose name, curiously enough, is King." She described the king as "grace and quiet in manner, with an honest, earnest look, like that of a man who thinks a good deal and does not talk much [with]... a good, kind look in his eyes." The man she was referring to was Padge King, whose image is on the previous page, along with his wife and son. After Mr. King came Eoin Concannon, Martin Oliver, Patrick Curran, and Mike Lynskey. It should be noted that as time has passed, the role of king has become largely ceremonial and he is no longer charged with leading an active fishing fleet. However, recent kings have all been proud representatives of the Claddagh at parades and great social occasions such as The Galway Races.

THE PEOPLE'S FOLK BELIEFS

The villagers' reliance on fishing shaped their way of life, leading to the strict adherence to numerous superstitions, which were known as *pishrogues* in the Irish tongue. Among these, it was considered extremely unlucky to handle any tool unrelated to fishing, such as farming implements like spades or ploughs; violators of this belief faced banishment from the village. Curiously, the mere presence of a red-haired woman or a hare on the path to the sea would promptly deter fishermen from embarking on their maritime journeys. To ensure a successful voyage, every boat departing for the sea had to carry oat-cake, salt, and ashes on board. Interestingly, the sight of a crow flying overhead and cawing was viewed as a favorable omen. While at sea, fishermen would refrain from naming four-legged animals, instead using the enigmatic term 'cold iron' to refer to them. Additionally, it was considered inappropriate to sing or play music aboard Claddagh sailing boats. When it came to medical matters, there were a number of distinctive cures in which the Claddagh people set great store. Cobwebs were placed on open sores or cuts. Poultices were applied to lumps and boils.

On a more poignant note, the Claddagh fishermen were especially protective of the swans of the Claddagh shore, who typically congregate near the Claddagh community hall. These elegant birds, like the fishermen of yore, would alternate time spent near the shoreline with forays out into the bay. It was believed that the swans contained the souls of long-dead fishermen who remained on this earth to watch over the boats of the Claddagh fleet.

THE DOMINICANS AND THE CLADDAGH

The presence of The Dominican Fathers in the Claddagh dates all the way back to 1488, when the Dominicans came from Athenry to the east of Galway and started their long association with the area. Their numbers varied throughout the centuries, as Penal Laws against Catholics were alternately imposed and then relaxed. However, by the early 19th century, the situation had stabilized, and a parish church was built. The Dominicans played a vital role both in the people's worldly concerns as well as in their spiritual welfare. It was the Dominicans who helped establish a primary school for the children of the area in 1846. This Piscatory (concerning fishing) school provided general education but also sought to introduce up-to-date fishing methods. However, over time it became a normal school and attempts to modernize the fishing industry met with little acceptance from the locals, who were firmly attached to their traditional ways.

The Dominicans also assisted fishermen in securing loans and generally being the people's advocates when it came to practical matters. In 1912, they were instrumental in the building of the Claddagh Hall. In this multi-purpose space, fishing tackle could be repaired and social functions held. To this day, it is one of the Dominican priests from the Claddagh who on a Sunday in the middle of August will sail forth, surrounded by other boats, for the centuries-old Blessing of the Bay. This unique occasion is when God's blessing is invoked on the fishing harvest, whose function nowadays is more a nod to the area's fishing heyday than any request for aid to the economic welfare of the current inhabitants of the Claddagh.

THE DECLINE OF THE CLADDAGH

'A letter from America', 1902

In the latter part of the 19th century, some poor fishing years and competition from well-financed, much larger steam trawlers further out in the bay set in motion the steady decline of the Claddagh's fishing economy. Deeply attached to their old customs, the fishermen spurned modern fishing techniques and clung tightly to their schedule of days when it was lucky and unlucky to fish. The 1847 potato famine took its toll on the Claddagh. In 1846, just 58 people were buried in the Claddagh cemetery. In what became known in Irish history as 'Black '47', a shocking 258 were buried, many due to cholera, which became a scourge in the wake of the famine. Many emigrated to the US after the famine, though immigrants did their best to send financial aid home to their families. The 'American letter,' in which news and updates would be accompanied by postal orders for however much money could be spared, was an essential part of the migration experience for people from many countries, but for none was it more important than the Irish. Between 1854 and 1875, authorities estimate that well over half of the more than 60 million letters mailed from the US to the UK were destined for Ireland, most written by young Irish women.

Many of the area's young men put their knowledge of the ocean to practical use and joined the British navy. Over time, the village's population dwindled and many of the characteristic thatched cottages with their whitewashed stone walls were left to fall into ruin as the inhabitants were forced to leave and seek their fortunes elsewhere. Several epidemics drew attention to the antiquated condition of the housing stock and discussions began about the need to replace the old homes with more efficient modern dwellings. In 1927, 255 Claddagh houses were surveyed, 51 were classed as 'poor', 69 as 'bad', and 106 as 'very bad.' There was much debate about the demolition of the old houses. Some suggested overhauling the existing cottages to make them more modern.

This call to modernize coincided with a decline in the fishing catches, as the fish were moving further out to sea, beyond the reach of the Claddagh fishing vessels. The shipping fleet declined rapidly from 68 boats to under 20. In 1930, John Connolly of the Urban District council said, "I remember when 60-80 fishing boats were in the Claddagh fleet. Today, only 6 or 8 are operating."

Many proposed keeping a certain number of cottages for their historical interest and as sites for tourists to visit. But the forces of "progress" prevailed and as Mrs. Grossman, a consulting American housing expert from St. Louis put it, "It is a great pity that these houses with their quiet charm should disappear. On the other hand, the insanitary conditions of the houses made them unfit for human habitation." And so, in the 1930s, almost all the thatched cottages were demolished to make way for efficient modern concrete dwellings. There were some holdouts, however, and the two final cottages, which belonged to Mrs. Maggie Halloran and Mrs. Bridie Molloy, were ultimately demolished in 1967 to make way for modern replacements.

THE CLADDAGH TODAY

The old Claddagh settlement of hundreds of whitewashed thatched cottages is now gone forever. However, traces of the past remain. Although different from the stone cottages past, the Claddagh's once-modern dwellings built in the 1930s have now themselves acquired a veneer of age. The pride people take in their gardens and homes today echoes the proud community of the past. Many of those who live there today trace their roots back generations. And those who have come in from outside remark on the friendly welcoming spirit that still pervades in the Claddagh. Visitors to the area can tour Katie's Cottage/Claddagh Arts Centre, where they can experience a recreated cottage interior decorated and equipped in authentic vintage style. There's also a striking Claddagh icon statue that pays homage to the past. Created by prominent Irish sculptor John Coll in 2009, the image of the Claddagh's iconic boat, the Hooker, is combined with that of a seabird and a sun that promises optimism.

Of course, the beating heart of the community is still the Dominican parish church on Claddagh Quay. As we learned earlier, it is one of these Dominicans who sets out to sea every August, surrounded by other fishing craft, for the touching ceremony of the Blessing of the Bay, to ensure safety and prosperity for all who fish those waters.

No matter how much the Claddagh has changed, the invigorating sea air and majestic views out over Galway Bay remain the same. The Galway Hooker Sailing Club make sure that the sight of this distinctive craft and its three sails are seen around Galway Bay. Needless to say, the Claddagh ring has spread the area's fame far and wide. Of course, places never truly leave their past behind. If you empty your mind, the spirits of the past may come flooding back and you might even be able to conjure up the lost village in your imagination. As author H.V. Morton put it in 1934,

"At night the Claddagh is most beautiful. There are no street lamps. You find your way through the maze of houses by the light that falls through windows and open doors. The path of earth has been beaten hard by the feet of generations going back to the Norman conquest of Ireland. The limewashed houses with the peat reek coming from their chimneys shine in the half light."

KATIE'S COTTAGE AND CLADDAGH ARTS CENTRE, 2023

Chapter Nine

A Symbol of Ireland
That Rivals the Flag and The Shamrock

For so many around the world with Irish roots, the Claddagh ring isn't just an ornamental trinket. It acts as a lifeline, linking them to their ancestral birthplace, offering a physical nod to a heritage deeply anchored in Ireland's verdant terrains and storied past. As those belonging to the diaspora traverse the complexities of blending in and reshaping identities, the ring remains a beacon of their origins. The massive migrations from Ireland, driven by hunger, economic struggles, and political upheavals, scattered the Irish to the remotest parts of the earth. In these unfamiliar places, amidst diverse cultures, the Claddagh ring emerged as a badge of one's roots.

This beautiful ring and its appeal has since moved beyond its initial role of signifying love or marriage to become a treasured legacy passed down through generations, with each bearer contributing to its unfolding narrative. In contemporary times, best men receive them from the groom, fathers bestow them upon their daughters, and its emblem, second only to the harp and the shamrock in representing Ireland, graces everything from shawls to backpacks, pins to ear studs and even graphic tees and body art. There is something universal about wishing that our hearts may be clasped by our beloved's embrace and that our lives are crowned with happiness. The Claddagh motif has become a versatile icon in contemporary style. It has been reimagined and infused into various types of adornments, including necklaces and earrings. Its appeal to celebrities, who frequently choose accessories with deep meaning, has further raised its profile in the realm of fashion. Individuals often choose Claddagh tattoos as a way to honor their Irish roots, celebrate a significant relationship, or to keep close at hand the virtues represented. The emblem has also sparked creativity across the art world, influencing a spectrum of artwork, from classic canvas works to contemporary digital creations, with each artist imparting their own interpretation of the enduring Irish symbol.

Chapter Ten

Famous People and Their Claddagh Rings

The Claddagh ring's charm transcends specific personalities or professions. Rooted in Irish heritage, it appeals to a broad spectrum of individuals, each weaving their own stories into its timeless emblem. From monarchs to musicians, the Claddagh ring's ageless motifs strike a chord, making it a beloved piece of jewelry for countless people. The tales of these notable individuals show what a profound impact this ring and its symbolism has had and continues to have.

APPROVAL FROM ROYALTY

Queen Victoria: The Claddagh ring found favor with Queen Victoria of England, perhaps surprising considering the turbulent and dark history between England and Ireland. In the 19th century, this Irish emblem was gifted to her, bestowing upon it royal prestige and subtly acknowledging Irish artistry and tradition.

Princess Grace and Prince Rainier of Monaco: The royal couple were presented with Claddagh-inspired jewelry in the form of a brooch and cufflinks. This gesture held special meaning for Grace Kelly, known for being proud of her Irish lineage. She even acquired a quaint cottage in County Mayo, once owned by her forebears, with dreams of renovating it as a holiday retreat. Unfortunately, this lovely dream remained unfulfilled due to her untimely passing.

ARISTOCRATIC PATRONAGE

Garech Browne, an heir to the Guinness brewing fortune: Browne, son of Lord Oranmore and Browne and his second wife Oonah, played a crucial role in preserving Irish culture and traditions. Not only did he assemble a collection of Claddagh rings that included the earliest surviving example (now to be seen at The Galway City Museum), but he also founded Claddagh Records in 1959, to preserve and promote traditional Irish music and the spoken word, including poetry, with such renowned Irish luminaries as Samuel Beckett, The Chieftains and Enya in its catalog. In his last will and testament, Browne left the City of Galway what are believed to be the historic gates of the old walled city, which had been previously transferred to his family's estate at Castle MacGarrett in Claremorris, County Mayo (the author's hometown!).

PRESIDENTIAL SEAL OF APPROVAL

Although we don't have an exhaustive record of what jewelry presidents and first ladies have worn down through the years, we do know of several instances of the Claddagh ring receiving the presidential seal of approval. John F. Kennedy, and his wife Jackie Kennedy, were known for their deep ties to their Irish roots. They bought Claddagh rings in Galway on a trip to Ireland just a few short months before President Kennedy was assassinated. And in more recent years, presidents Reagan and Clinton were both presented with Claddagh rings.

STARS OF STAGE AND SCREEN

Walt Disney: The mastermind behind Disney's enchanting universe, Walt Disney, proudly acknowledged his Irish lineage through the Claddagh ring. Statues of Disney at Disneyland and a wax figure at Madame Tussauds in Orlando depict him wearing this ring. Purchased during a trip to Ireland in the early 60s for the world premiere of *Darby O'Gill and the Little People*, it was the only ring he wore other than his wedding band.

Jim Morrison: The iconic frontman of The Doors had a special connection with the Claddagh ring. Morrison and his beloved, Patricia Kennealy, exchanged these rings in a Celtic commitment ritual.

U2: Contemporary rock stars have also been known to wear a Claddagh ring. Both Bono and Adam Clayton have been seen wearing them. There are even accounts of Bono drawing an image of a Claddagh ring on a fan's arm, adding a B below to complete the "autograph."

Vampires?!: Bram Stoker, the creator of *Dracula*, was a Dublin man. We wonder what he'd think of all the vampire tales spawned by his novel of 1897. In particular, what would he have thought of *Buffy the Vampire Slayer*? Well, the Claddagh ring received worldwide attention when writer/director Joss Whedon used its meaning as a recurring theme in the plot of the famous television series. Its symbolism became a central plot device when male lead, Angel, gifted Buffy with a Claddagh ring and explained, "My people - before I was changed - they exchanged this as a sign of devotion. It's a Claddagh ring."

Bond, James Bond: A shiny Claddagh ring was spotted on the finger of Shirley Eaton when she played the famous Bond Girl Jill Masterson in a 1964 James Bond film. Which Bond film, you might ask? Why, *Goldfinger* (with its emphasis on precious metals), of course! Apparently, as Shirley Bassey stridently sang in the film's theme song, "She *LOVED* gold!!" In the book written by Ian Fleming, it's pointed out that Jill Masterson's ring may have been missing the crown, and that due to the lack of this symbol of loyalty, she was not to be trusted. This was indeed accurate as it turned out she had been the 'friend and acquaintance' of the evil Ernest

Blofeld before she fell for the debonair Mr. Bond, played in the film by none other than Sean Connery.

Kladdagh!:Kanye West and Kim Kardashian are said to have bought Claddagh rings as a memento of a trip to Ireland. Neither has been spotted wearing them, but now that they're no longer a couple, one wonders if wearing their rings could have helped them stay together! If you can't afford to emulate their lavish lifestyle and "keep up with the Kardashians," most budgets will stretch to a Claddagh ring, as they come in many variations, both deluxe and more modest versions.

Chapter Eleven

The Future of The Claddagh Ring

The late 19th and early 20th centuries heralded a pivotal era for the Claddagh ring. As members of the Irish diaspora ventured to distant lands, particularly the United States, the ring's prominence expanded internationally. It emerged as a symbol of pride among the Irish immigrants in America. During this period, design innovations saw the heart occasionally replaced with birthstones or the addition of intricate Celtic patterns to accentuate its Irish heritage. The ring's symbolism began captivating a wider audience, extending beyond its initial cultural confines.

As societies have progressed and traditions evolved, the Claddagh ring has demonstrated a remarkable ability to remain relevant. In today's world, where individuality is prized, we can see even more variations of this ring. These include pioneering materials, eco-friendly sources, or even tech-infused features. Contemporary takes on the Claddagh ring often reimagine the conventional heart, hands, and crown arrangement, opting for updated design principles. Moreover, the Claddagh's enduring motif has diversified, appearing on apparel and even as tattoos.

Yet, the central message of the Claddagh ring endures. Its signature elements - the hands, heart, and crown, symbolizing friendship, affection, and loyalty - possess an enduring charm that few emblems can rival. While its roots are deeply anchored in Irish tales and customs, its resonance is global. This iconic ring has journeyed across ages, regions, and diverse human narratives, maintaining its irresistible appeal. For its bearers, it serves as an affirmation of affection, a mark of ancestry, an artistic expression, and occasionally, a connection to forebears never known. Amidst a swiftly evolving landscape, the Claddagh ring is destined to be a testament to true love for generations to come.

The Claddagh Boatman

- A TRADITIONAL SONG

I am a Claddagh boatman bold,

Quite humble is my calling,

From morn 'til night,

From dark 'til light,

Round Galway Bay I'm trawling.

I care not for the great man's frown,

I ask not for his favour,

My wants are few,

No debts I've due

I live by honest labour.

I have one son a gallant boy,

Not stained by spot, nor speckle,

He pulls and hauls

And works the trawls,

And keeps right trim the tackle.

His father trained his son to be,

Hard working, honest, manly,

The sagart [Irish for 'priest'] says round Galway Bay,

There's none like young Matt Hanely.

I have thank God a girl as good,

Dear Eileen, slight and slender,

She works and mends,

And brightens home

With love that's bright and tender.

When Sunday brings that hour of rest,

That sweet relief from labour,

We crossed the fields in friendly groups,

And gossiped with our neighbours.

We and they, put in the day,

With harmless recreation

Could Erin's sons live their lives

And need no emigration.

Chapter Twelve

Learning More About
the Claddagh Ring and The Claddagh

2023 VIEW OF THOMAS DILLON CLADDAGH GOLD, 2023,
ORIGINAL MAKERS OF THE CLADDAGH RING

I hope you've learned a lot about the Claddagh ring and enjoyed adding to your store of knowledge about this remarkable piece of jewelry and the place that gave this symbol of love and Irish heritage its name, the Galway fishing village of the Claddagh.

If you'd like to continue your reading on the topic, this book's bibliography lists the sources I used in my research.

If you'd like to go even further on your scholarly journey, take a look at the information below for The Claddagh Ring Museum, the Galway Museum, The Claddagh Arts Centre, and Galway City Walking Tours. Who knows? Maybe one day you'll get to visit them in person and even take a stroll along the shore of The Claddagh, taking in those invigorating breezes that blow across Galway Bay.

The Claddagh Ring Musuem at Thomas Dillion's Claddagh Gold
claddaghring.ie
tel: +353 91 566365
email:info@claddaghring.ie
1 Quay Street, Galway, Ireland

An absolute must-see if you're in Galway. Thomas Dillon's shop is the oldest jewelers in Ireland and the original maker of the Claddagh ring since 1750. Any rings bought from this shop have a certificate of authenticity. As well as being a retail premises with very fine Claddagh rings and other Claddagh jewelry, they also house a small museum with a large history. On display are some of the very first Claddagh rings in existence, as well as "the world's smallest Claddagh ring that fits on the top of a pin." You can see the tools used to make Claddagh rings and learn about the various stages of production. If that isn't enough, there are vintage photographs of Galway and relics from the Stone Age and the 1847 potato famine. The owner is an avid historian and a welcoming gentleman in the best Galway fashion. The best part is that while you're waiting to visit Galway, you can order your Claddagh rings on their website from the comfort of your home.

The Galway City Museum
https://galwaycitymuseum.ie/
tel: +353 91 532 460
email: museum@galwaycity.ie
Spanish Parade, Galway H91 CX5P

The Galway Museum, located just beside the Spanish Arch, offers an incredible Claddagh exhibit upstairs. The oldest surviving Claddagh ring is included in their collection. Numerous images, works of art, essays, relics, and more about the renowned historic small village can also be found here. You can even get a taste of some special Claddagh exhibits online: (https://galwaycitymuseum.ie/virtual-tour/). Especially fascinating is the fact that the museum overlooks the Claddagh and a particular viewing point will show you the location and backstory of various sections of the Claddagh, such as where certain activities were carried out, who lived where, and much more!

Wild Atlantic Workshop & Katie's Claddagh Cottage
https://www.facebook.com/CladdaghArtsCentre/
+ 353 85 196 8022 (ring or text Elizabeth for bookings)
+ 353 87 8280848 (general inquiries)
claddaghcottagecrafts@gmail.com
IMPORTANT NOTE: pre-booking is essential to avoid disappointment.

This re-creation of a Claddagh cottage is a welcoming, family-run enterprise. Located in the heart of the old fishing community, it offers a step back in time to help us envision what life was like in a humble Irish fisherman's cottage of the old Claddagh. Unfortunately, the original community of stone cottages was demolished in the 1930s, but this is an authentic re-creation of what used to be there. It was lovingly constructed by owner Cathriona Walsh with the help of her father, who grew up in one of the original cottages. The local Claddagh community generously donated many of the tools, clothing, and artifacts on display. This cottage is small in size, like the original cottages, and doesn't have the big echoing halls of a traditional museum. There aren't extensive scholarly displays or glass-topped cases, but it offers visitors a chance to get a sense of how life was lived in the Claddagh. You'll also be treated to delicious Irish tea and scones! It's not always open, though, so be sure to call ahead and make reservations.

Galway City Walking Tours
https://www.galwaywalks.com
Brian Nolan
+ 353 86 3273560
galwaywalks@gmail.com
Twitter: @galwaywalks

These tours were established over 20 years ago by Brian Nolan, a tourism professional with many years of travel experience in Ireland and the US. Brian is a highly knowledgeable local historian with a compelling way of explaining and bringing Ireland's history to life. He comes highly recommended for his unique blend of wit and wisdom. As he puts it himself, "It's not about the city, it's about the people who lived and died here…it's their stories I love to tell."

Chapter Thirteen

Write Your Own Claddagh Ring Story

In this little book, I've tried to share some history, stories and legends associated with the Claddagh ring. While writing it, I was honored that so many, many people shared with me how much a Claddagh ring has meant to them.

Bearing that in mind, I realized that you may wish to treasure this book as a keepsake for you or for your family. The following pages are here for you to write your story about your own Claddagh ring and what it has meant to you.

You may wish to write about how you came to have your ring or how you gave a Claddagh ring to somebody close to you. Was there an interesting tale attached to how you bought it or how it came into your possession? What associations does it conjure up in your mind? Does it make you think about Ireland?

Perhaps when you look at it on your finger you think of your own family. Does it revive sweet memories of days gone by?

Feel free to tell your story so you can re-read it in the future or even share it with others...

_____

_____

_____

_____

_____

_____

_____

_____

_____

_____

_____

_____

_____

_____

_____

_____

_____

_____

_____

Could You Help Me?

ENJOYED THIS BOOK? YOU CAN MAKE A REAL DIFFERENCE!

Reviews are the most powerful tool when it comes to getting the word out about my books. I would love to be able to promote a book like the big publishing houses, but I'm just a one-man operation and can't take out full-page ads in the newspapers like they do. However, I do have a treasured resource that these publishers would do anything to get their hands on:

A kind and loyal group of readers who aren't afraid to share the love...

Sincere, honest reviews that come from the heart bring my books to the attention of other readers, who will hopefully enjoy them just as much.

If this book brought you a few moments of pleasure, I'd be forever grateful if you took a few minutes out of your busy day to leave a review (even just a couple of words would be appreciated) on the book's Amazon page.

You can get to the review page simply by scanning the QR code below.

Thanks! (Go raibh maith agat)

About The Author and Publisher

From the west of Ireland, but now living in New York, I enjoy sharing tales of Irish history with those I meet. Whether it's fascinating Irish trivia or unusual tales of Ireland that few people know, I spend a great deal of time scouring vintage newspaper articles, dusty old books and listening to tales of the older generations in Ireland. It's my pleasure to share that knowledge with my readers. That's why I set up my little publishing imprint, *Mullarkey's Books of Ireland*. No matter how far back your Irish connection is, I know we all feel a sense of belonging with that wind-tossed isle in the Atlantic, home to stirring tales of bravery and the heritage of decent hardworking people making their way in a world that wasn't always easy. If you ever want to contact me directly, please email plainscribespress@gmail.com. And, of course, don't forget to follow me on Amazon for details of my latest books about Ireland. Just scan the link on the following page...

Séamus Mullarkey,
Founder, MULLARKEY'S BOOKS OF IRELAND

Follow Me

...THERE'S LOTS MORE TO COME...

Scan the code so you

get notified the minute I release a new book...

SCAN TO FOLLOW ME...

Disclaimer

This book is for entertainment purposes only. Under no circumstances will any legal responsibility or blame be held against the publisher for any reparation, damages, or monetary loss due to the text or images herein, either directly or indirectly. Every effort has been made to ensure the historical accuracy of the information contained herein. However, due to the incompleteness and sometimes contradictory nature of historical sources, no attestations are made to claim complete historical accuracy.

Bibliography

Delamer, Ida (1996). "The Claddagh Ring". *Irish Arts Review*. 12: 181–187.

George Quinn. (1970) *The Claddagh Ring, The Mantle*, 13:9–13.

James Hardiman (1820), *The History of the Town and County of the Town of Galway*,

William Dillon. (1906) *Journal of the Galway Archaeological and Historical Society*, 5.

Seán McMahon. (2005) *Story of the Claddagh Ring*, Mercier Press, Cork, Ireland.

Peadar O'Dowd,(1993) *Down by the Claddagh*, Kenny's Bookshop & Art Gallery

Malachy McCourt (2004) *The Claddagh Ring*, Running Press

Cecily Joyce, (1991) *The Claddagh Ring Story*, Clodoiri Lurgan Teo

Mary Banim, (1892) *Here and There Through Ireland*, Freeman's Journal

H. V. Morton,, (1934) *In Search of Ireland*, Methuen

Mr and Mrs. Hall, (1840), *Tour of Ireland*, How & Parsons

Images

--gift page, sketch of Claddagh ring, author's own

--before preface, photo of gold Claddagh on text background free to use under wikicommons license

--'Irish grandmother' author's sketch

--'fede ring' author's own photograph

--'large Claddagh ring' author's own sketch-meaning of heart, hands, crown

--sketch of how to wear Claddagh ring, author's own sketch

--photograph, Garech Browne collection, public domain

--ad for Dillon's Claddagh rings, public domain

--Claddagh's legendary legacy, sketch, author's own

--Legend #1, sketch, author's own

--Legend #2 sketch, author's own

--Ordnance Survey map, 1838-1840, public domain

--vintage Claddagh stereoscope image, public domain, 1860s (public domain, picryl)

--row of fishermen's cottages in Claddagh, stereoscope image, (public domain, picryl)

--photograph, Galway Hooker, Maura Mullarkey, free to use

--Girl of the Claddagh, drawing 1855, (public domain, picryl)

--Blessing of the Bay, sketch author's own, inspired by vintage print

--street vendors, The Quays, 1902, public domain

--Two Claddagh Fishermen, 19th Century, Sketch, author's Own, Inspired by vintage photograph

--closeup detail from postcard titled "Catch of the Day," between 1900 and 1909, public domain

--image of Claddagh rings against petals, (public domain, picryl)

--Claddagh king, Padneen King, sketch author's own, inspired by vintage photograph

--photograph of swan, photograph, Maura Mullarkey, free to use

--Dominican church, sketch, author's own, inspired by vintage photograph

--vintage photograph, letter from America, public domain

-- photograph, author's own, Katie's cottage

--Claddagh ring hanging sign, wikicommons, public domain

--photograph, girl with hands clasped, Giulia Bertelli, free to use under Unsplash licence

--photograph, Thomas Dillon Claddagh Gold shop and museum, photograph, author's own

--Claddagh rings, against flowers, (public domain, picryl)

A VERY SPECIAL **FREE** BONUS!

Do you want to learn more about Ireland?

Interesting and Unusual Ireland can be yours for FREE…

This BONUS book has fascinating trivia, interesting tales and compelling stories about Ireland that you won't find elsewhere…

DOWNLOAD YOUR COPY <u>FOR FREE</u> SO YOU CAN LEARN ALL ABOUT IRELAND

NOTES

NOTES

NOTES

NOTES

NOTES

NOTES

NOTES

Made in the USA
Middletown, DE
06 December 2023

44857421R00066